D1487649

101 Ways to Market Your Online Jewelry Shop

This book is designed for online jewelry shop owners, but all jewelry shop owners will find some creative, original ideas that can work for their business.

Almost all the ideas in this book are free or cheap to put into action. Even if some of the ideas don't appeal to you, there are 101, so you'll find at least a few that will increase your profits.

In this book, you'll see some references to a site called Etsy.com. This website allows you to set up shop with your handcrafted items. It currently has over 1.8 million users and 200,000 sellers. I recommend it for all crafters who want to reach a wider audience.

Okay. Grab your highlighter and let's get to the fun stuff.

OFFER ONE PRIZE IN EVERY 10 SHIPMENTS

Make a large banner or announcement that lets people know that you ship one great prize in every 10 shipments. You can tell them what the prize is or make it a secret.

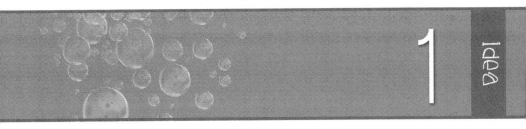

This makes buying from you a lot more fun, and sets you apart from competitors. And think of all the great testimonials you'll get from the people who win the prize. They'll definitely tell their friends and family about it if they win something, and that's more business for you.

Consider making a winners page on your website, with photos of your customers with their prize. The prize winners will be sure to send the link to all their friends and family.

MAIL POSTCARDS TO MAGAZINES

Can you imagine the exposure you would get if you were featured in a magazine? You can make that happen!

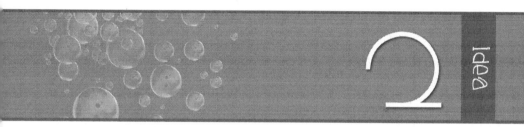

idea 2

Get a few images of your products printed onto postcards from an online printer (vistaprint.com and overnightprints.com are good options) and address them to 6-12 magazines, with a message that includes a little about your shop and your shop address. You can also tell them you'd be glad to send samples if they're interested in featuring some of your jewelry.

Remember, magazine writers and editors are really busy and even if you have wonderful jewelry that they'd be interested in, they're not likely to be able to find your site and contact you out of the blue. You have to contact them instead of waiting for them to come to you.

WRITE A CHILDREN'S BOOK

You can write a short children's story and use a specific jewelry as one of the main points of interest in the story. For example, you could write a story about a little girl who loses her bunny locket, and the story could revolve around her search for her locket. The possibilities for story ideas are endless.

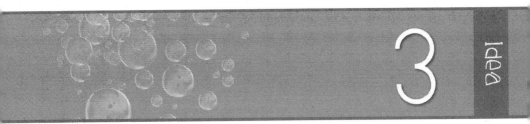

3

Idea

Have an online printer print your storybook (you can get them really cheap if you're on a budget) and just include the cost of the book in the total of the order. Then include the book with the locket and sell it as a set.

This would make a really great gift set for a little girl!

COLLABORATE WITH AN ARTIST

Give the artist some jewelry to work with, and have them make a sculpture or some other type of art with it. Have the artist record the process on a camcorder or webcam, speed it up, and then post it on YouTube, with links to both your site and the artist's site.

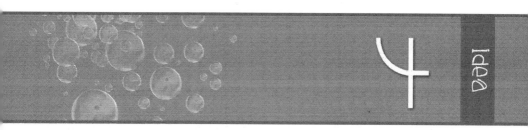

You could also lend the piece to a boutique or any other small business in exchange for them displaying your website info on a card beneath the sculpture. If it's nice-looking, it will definitely attract visitors into their shop, so they'll be happy to display it.

CUTESY BOX ALTERNATIVES

Wouldn't it be cute to give a necklace as a gift, wrapped around a little stuffed bear's neck?

Idea

5

Offer this as an add-on and show a picture in your listing. You could also consider using stuffed bunnies or hippos, depending on the preferences of your customers. It may not seem like much, but if you get a few more sales from busy women who want to give a cute gift and don't have time to do some creative wrapping themselves, isn't it worth it?

MAIL BROCHURES TO BOUTIQUES

If you're interested in selling your jewelry at cheaper prices for large orders, you can make up some small brochures (they don't have to be elaborate) and mail them to independent boutiques locally or across the nation.

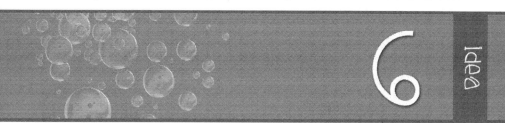

6

Idea

Be sure and put your website address on them and your contact information. It's also a good idea to let them know the pricing so that they don't have to contact you to see if your products are in their budget.

You could also include an order form with the brochures for those who aren't big fans of the internet.

LEND JEWELRY TO SCHOOL THEATERS

If the local high school is putting on a play, you can lend them some of your jewelry to be worn with the costumes.

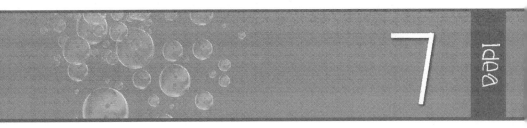

7

Idea

You can leave fliers or cards at the ticket booth that tell people that the actors are wearing your jewelry and list your website address so they can get their own.

It's a good idea to include a coupon that expires in a week so they'll act quickly and won't forget.

BOOKMARKS

Design some pretty bookmarks or have a professional graphic designer do it for you. Graphic designers on Etsy.com are very cheap and most of them are very good, and the price range for this type of design would only cost 10-25 dollars.

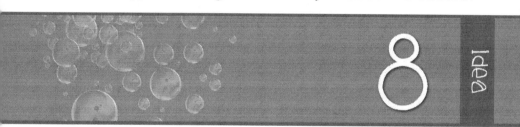

Be sure and put some pictures of your jewelry on the bookmark, your website address, and maybe a coupon code.

Give the bookmarks away to libraries and bookstores or leave stacks of them on college campuses and libraries. Or hire a girl to hand them out at her high school or college.

JEWELRY + SOAP

Collaborate with soap makers and have them make soap bars with your jewelry inside. Once the soap dwindles down to nothing, the gift recipient will have their jewelry.

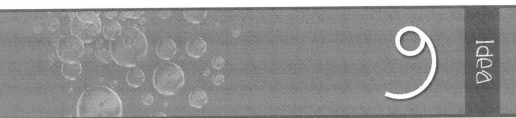

This would make an exciting gift that definitely beats just a regular bar of soap.

You can target these at parents of little girls by making childrens jewelry and having the soap maker use shapes like hearts or horses.

BE OUTRAGEOUS FOR ATTENTION

Make a really outrageous piece of jewelry, either in size, expense, or looks. Then post it on your site and let everyone know it's there.

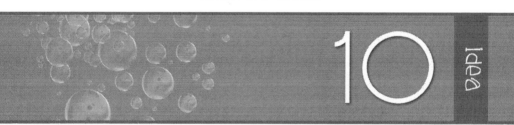

Wouldn't you take a look if someone sent you a link titled, "Crazy Weird Electronic Necklace" or "World's Longest Necklace" or "Color-Changing Earrings"? And since they're already there, a good portion of them will take a look at your other (less weird) jewelry.

POST YOUR OUTRAGEOUS JEWELRY ON YOUTUBE

When making your outrageous jewelry piece, record yourself doing it on your webcam or camcorder, and then speed the video up and post it on YouTube. People love watching other people's speed crafting videos.

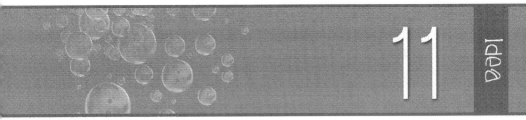

11

Idea

Once it's up on YouTube, you can embed it onto your own website and let everyone know to come check it out.

OFFER CUSTOM JEWELRY

Many times I've seen a great piece of jewelry that I'd like to buy, if only it had one minor change to it. I never ask because I'm afraid of insulting the artist.

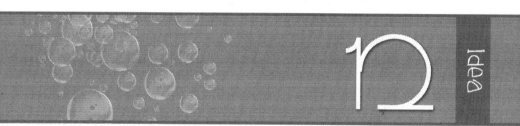

Let people know they can have changes made to the jewelry they see or you can make completely custom jewelry – most people are just too afraid of offending you to ask.

PULL AN AVON

Make your own catalogs and recruit salespeople. Pay a percentage of the earnings in exchange for them selling your products for you.

13

Idea

You can increase sales exponentially without any extra work on your part, except mailing out the jewelry.

OFFER 3 DAY SHIPPING AT NO EXTRA CHARGE

This may not work for everyone, but go to your post office and see how much more it would cost for you to ship something 3 day compared to regular ground shipping.

14 Idea

Normally the cost is only a few cents more. If so, offer two day shipping at no extra charge, and you'll see a lot more sales for it.

JEWELRY IN A BALLOON

Put your jewelry inside a soft pouch or bag and put that inside a balloon and fill it with helium. Then put the blown up balloon inside a box.

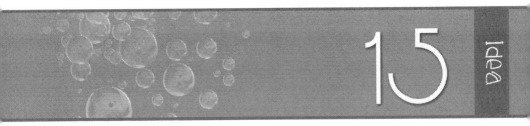

15

Idea

Now, when the recipient opens the box, the balloon will fly up a few feet with your jewelry inside. You can write "Thanks! Your Jewelry is Inside!" on the balloon.

Warning: This will only work on expedited shipments – otherwise, the helium will seep out of the balloon before it's opened.

PROMOTIONAL MODELS

You can hire promotional models for $8-$13 an hour to work at festivals or other events and hand out your fliers, bookmarks, or stickers. Just post on craigslist.org under gigs – events.

16 Idea

Or you can be your own promotional model. Go out with your family and friends and pass out all your promotional items. Watch how quickly people will line up to get your free stuff.

BOOK COVERS

A huge portion of jewelry-buyers are teenage girls. Teenage girls go to school, and most schools require book covers on all school textbooks.

17

Idea

Design a gorgeous bookcover with your jewelry featured on it and then give them away to school girls. This will amount to an enormous amount of exposure to a demographic that spends a lot of money on jewelry.

This website has some reasonable prices on custom book covers: www.westsky.com/bookcovers.htm

CONTACT NUMBER

Did you know that by including a contact number on your site, you will increase trust, sales, and pagerank? Google puts sites that include a contact number higher on search results than sites that don't.

18

Idea

If you don't want to give out your personal contact number, you can get an account on Skype.com for $2.95 a month that lets you send or receive unlimited calls worldwide on your computer, and you can get your own Skype phone number for only $13 for three months. If you're not available, callers will get sent to your Skype voicemail. So for about $7 a month, you can have your own business number.

CELEBRITY LINE

Are there any celebrities whose jewelry style you really admire? You can base an entire line of your jewelry on that celebrity's style. It's almost like having a famous actress advertise for you.

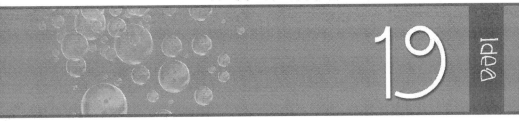

19

Idea

Think about all the girls out there that want to dress just like Angelina Jolie or Audrey Hepburn. You can make that possible and make a tidy profit in the process.

CATEGORIZE BY STYLE AND BY PRODUCT

When someone is searching for jewelry, they're first looking for a style, and secondly looking for a product. Even if I'm looking for necklaces, I'd rather see a whole page of earrings that are my style than a whole page of necklaces that are not.

20 idea

You can list by age: Child, Teen, Adult. You can list by activity: Evening Out, Casual Day, Office Wear. There are lots of other ways to list your product. Just make sure people have another way of finding products than by categories like "necklaces" and "earrings."

LATEST TRENDS SECTION

Offer a section of your jewelry shop site or Etsy shop to Latest Trends. Devote this section to jewelry that's extra fashionable at the moment for those fashion bugs.

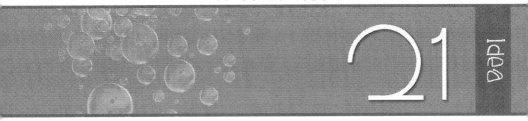

21

Idea

You're more likely to be picked up in blogs and social networking sites if you offer trendy products.

POST IN FORUMS

Post in forums, but don't spam. Post useful information and make friends.

If you post a link to your site under each of your posts, you'll definitely get some free exposure.

HIT UP HIGH SCHOOL GIRLS

Offer to let high school girls wear your jewelry in exchange for them taking your business cards (preferably with a coupon code on the back) to their school and handing them to anyone who compliments them on the jewelry.

23

idea

This will work best with more popular girls or girls with great style.

CREATE A JEWELRY BLOG

Make a blog about your jewelry or jewelry in general or celebrity jewelry, or whatever you want, as long as it relates to jewelry. Make it interesting with helpful advice and coupons, and be sure and update it consistently or you'll lose readers.

24 idea

Wordpress is a great blog option that gets really high Google rank within hours. For example, if you made a blog post titled, "How to Get Angelina Jolie's Jewelry Style" and searched Google 6-24 hours later for the words "angelina jolie jewelry style," your blog would be one of the top listings.

Don't overstuff with keywords and just write naturally.

CAR MAGNETS

You can get tons of exposure if you drive. Vistaprint.com offers large car magnets at really cheap prices. Have one made with a photo of your jewelry and your site address and stick it on the side of your car.

You could even offer a coupon code on it so you would know how many people found your site from your car magnet.

This small investment will get you exposure for years and years.

YAHOO ANSWERS

Yahoo Answers is a site where people type in a question and have it answered by anyone else in the community who wants to answer. It's really easy and free.

26

idea

When someone asks a question about jewelry, just pop in with your answer and a link to your website. Sometimes Yahoo Answer pages get very high Google pagerank and sometimes streams of people will find you from a question you answered a year ago.

answers.yahoo.com

POST COMMENTS ON BLOGS

60% of readers also read the comments. Just make sure you're not spamming (spam comments look like this: Nice post. Go look at my site at www.example.com.) and make sure you're posting in blogs that attract the right demographic.

27

Idea

The majority of jewelry-buyers are females who are at least somewhat fashion conscious. So a good place to post would be fashion, makeup, or celebrity blogs.

PRINT PAMPHLETS

Design some pamphlets with your products and website listed inside and leave stacks of them with local restaurants, boutiques, or other shops that target the same demographic that you do.

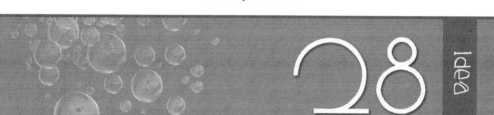

28

Idea

Don't forget to include coupons and refer-a-friend discounts.

HOLIDAY BANNER

Many times I've gone to Google on a holiday solely to see what new graphic they put up for that day. If you consistently change your banner or logo on holidays, and it's creative and fun, people will want to come see it. And the more visitors to your shop, the better.

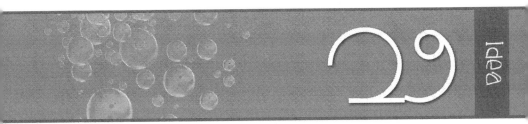

Customers will even tell their friends to go check it out before it's gone. Easy traffic!

PAYMENT OPTIONS

Offer as many payment options as possible to avoid losing customers. If you accept cash, check, money order, Paypal, and credit/debit cards, you have everyone covered.

Make sure you prominently display the payment options somewhere on your site. When I used to only pay with Paypal online, I would automatically leave an online store that didn't show the Paypal symbol on their order page.

BLOGGER REVIEWS

Ask bloggers of high ranking blogs (make sure they get plenty of visitors in your target demographic) if you can send them a few jewelry items for them to review on their blog.

31

Idea

You'll get tons of exposure from people who trust the writer's opinion and will have more faith in you.

WRITE ARTICLES

If you have knowledge about jewelry – how to make jewelry, what kind of jewelry looks good with what kind of clothes, health benefits of gemstones, etc. – you can write articles about your expertise and submit it to blogs or websites that would be interested in posting it.

32

idea

You can put your name and a link to your website at the bottom of the article and watch the traffic come streaming in.

BACKLINKS

If you've implemented the last two ideas, you now have back-links. Backlinks are links to your website from other quality websites. They are crucial to rising to the top of Google.

There are some important things you need to know about backlinks, though:

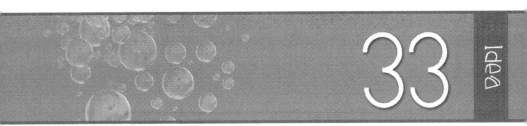

Don't get too many backlinks at one time. Five backlinks per week is the maximum; otherwise Google might suspect you of dubious activity and will greatly lower your pagerank.

Don't buy backlinks. The sites that link-sellers put your link on will not give you higher pagerank because they're not quality sites. Also, they overload the web with your links all at once, which will cause Google to lower your pagerank dramatically.

So try to get links to your site on the highest ranked sites you can. But don't overdo it.

NEWSLETTERS

Put an opt-in form on your site that allows people to sign up for your mailing list/newsletter.

34

Idea

Don't send these out too often. Once a month is a good idea.

You can include any news about your business, coupons, new items, or sales.

GETTING YOUTUBERS TO ADVERTISE FOR YOU

Ask popular YouTubers if you can send them some samples of your jewelry and write on the box, "Please Open This On Camera." Some of the most popular YouTubers are young people who love to get little surprises, and they don't normally get gifts even when they have enormous YouTube popularity.

35
Idea

You can ask them to put a link to your site in the sidebar, but they'll most likely do that without having to be asked.

DONATE

Donate a few of your jewelry items to school or scout raffles or to charity auctions.

36 idea

Make sure you attach a tag with your site address on the jewelry. Many times they will offer you free advertising at the charity event for your donations, too.

BUSINESS CARD COUPONS

Make up a set of business cards, but make them into coupons.

37 Idea

Put a dotted line around the edges so people immediately recognize that it's a coupon.

You can put these in libraries, bookstores, and anywhere else that has a spot for promotional papers.

ENTER CONTESTS

Be on the lookout for art or jewelry contests that you can enter your work into.

38

idea

If you win or become a finalist, you'll get tons of free exposure and an award you can add to your bio.

Here's one to look at:
jtvdesigncontest.com

FORUMS

Post helpful comments on forums related to jewelry, fashion, or woman-related issues.

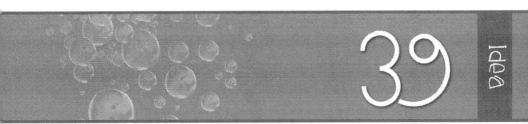

39 Idea

In your profile section, you will have the option to add a signature – in that section, just put a link to your website that explains what you sell.

This can get you fast exposure if it's a popular forum.

START YOUR OWN FAN CLUB

At groups.yahoo.com you can create a fan club group for your own site. It has a forum and mailing list already built in.

You can write a message and just hit "send to group" and send the message to the entire group.

On your fan club group, you can offer coupons just for fan club member, new items, sale information, and monthly gifts.

TEAM UP

Join forces with other online sellers who have the same style as you but different products.

You can include coupons or fliers for each others' sites with every shipment you send out.

idea 41

If you team up with a clothing seller, art seller, soap seller, candle seller, and purse seller, you'll get tons of exposure to the right demographic, and a group of people that are spending money, for free, besides the cost of the fliers.

EXTRA BROCHURES

If you use brochures when you ship out items, include extra ones with coupons in them for your customer's friends.

You can also offer an incentive (20% off their next order) if a friend they've referred orders from you.

AFFILIATE PROGRAMS

You can set up an affiliate program that allows other people to sell your product for you in exchange for commission.

For example, an affiliate marketer would make his own ads and promote your products himself, and whenever you sold a product because of his promotions, he would get 20-50% of the profit.

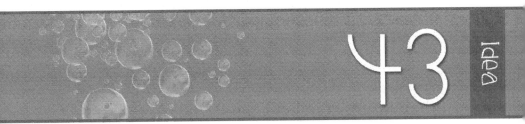

43 Idea

You decide how much you pay affiliates and you can end your affiliate program at any time.

Here's some more information on affiliate programs:
www.web-source.net/affiliate_program.htm

THANK YOU NOTES

Send thank you notes to your best customers a week or two after you ship their order.

44

idea

This will remind them of your shop and they'll probably take a look around to see if you have anything new to offer.

CD BROCHURES

Wouldn't it be neat to give out a CD instead of a brochure?

You can make videos of your product in Windows Movie Maker and put them on the CD and hand those out when people ask about your jewelry.

Or leave them for free at the register of boutiques or flower shops.

You can get a pack of 50 CDs for 13.50 at Amazon.com.

RESEARCH PREFERENCES

You probably have a good idea of what you like and what those around you like, but when you sell online, you have to know what people around the country or world like.

46

idea

Polls are a great way to find out, and the best place for polls is buzzdash.com. Just type in the buzzdash search entries like: jewelry, earrings, gems, etc. and you'll find information on people's preferences that you can incorporate into your business.

RESEARCH KEYWORDS

Another good research tool is the Google Keyword Tool
(adwords.google.com/select/KeywordToolExternal).

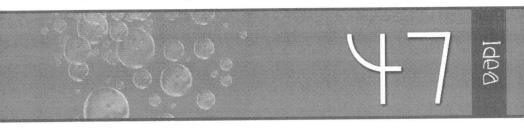

47 Idea

It allows you to check how many times any specific
keyword was typed into Google that month, and the
average of previous months.

So let's say you're trying to decide between making a line of
anklets or a line of toe rings. You can search, "anklets" and
"toe rings" to see which received higher searches that month.
In case you're wondering, for the month of October, anklets
are slightly more popular.

HOLD A CONTEST

Put a contest on your website with a great prize from your jewelry collection and let as many people know about it as possible. You can have a contest for a new slogan or a new banner.

48

Idea

You can have the contest winner be decided by votes, and people will definitely tell their friends and family to go to the site to vote, which means lots of visitors for you.

EMAIL MAGAZINES AND NEWSPAPERS

If you've come up with something really exciting or different for your business, email editors at magazines and newspapers and tell them about it.

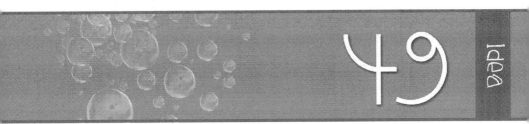

49

Idea

They might write a story about you and your business, which would result in massive free exposure.

PRESS RELEASES

If you're not comfortable sending emails to editors, you can always write up a press release and submit it to prweb.com or prnewswire.com.

50 Idea

These are press release websites, and they're where journalists and news editors go to find new stories. If they like your press release, they'll contact you!

Here's some free information on how to write a press release: www.wikihow.com/Write-a-Press-Release

SQUIDOO

If you're going to write articles about jewelry-related topics, or if you just want to write flat-out advertisement articles, you can use Squidoo.com.

51

Idea

Squidoo gets very high pagerank on Google, and they're the only article site that will allow you to write obvious advertisements, and it's free.

You can connect all your pages on Squidoo (they're called lenses) so that people can navigate through all your articles easily.

CREATE A FREQUENT BUYER PROGRAM

Make a program for your business that allows people to get $10 off once they've purchased $100 or $200 worth of merchandise.

52 idea

Many times, I've spent an extra $30 just to get my $10 off coupon.

UNBIRTHDAY SURPRISE

If you've ever watched Disney's Alice in Wonderland, you remember the scene where Alice meets Mad Hatter and March Hare in the middle of an unbirthday party.

53
Idea

Send out unbirthday cards to your customers instead of the usual birthday cards, and give them a coupon or some other promotional items as a gift.

ESTABLISH YOURSELF AS AN EXPERT

If you've been implementing the steps advising you to write articles and a blog, you've already started establishing yourself as an expert in your field.

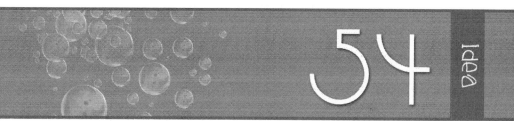

54 Idea

Because of this, your name will get higher pagerank when used in unison with your keywords, buyers will trust you more, and editors will trust you more, which are all important in getting exposure and making sales.

If you want to take this further, you can write on wikihow.com, write eBooks, or even regular books, and have them self-published. All of these help further your image as an expert.

DIGG

Digg is a site that allows people to recommend sites they like to other Digg users.

55

Idea

You can go to Digg.com and "digg" your own site. This is allowed, but make sure you use proper keyword tags and an accurate description.

This can offer an immediate spike of traffic to your site.

STUMBLE UPON

StumbleUpon.com is a site very similar to Digg, but you should also post your site here, because many people only use Digg OR StumbleUpon and not both.

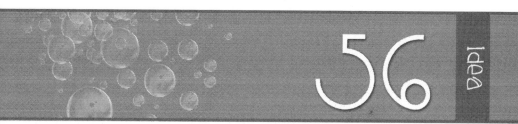

56 | idea

You'll have to download a small toolbar to use StumbleUpon, but it's definitely worth it for the huge traffic spike.

ABOUT ME SECTION

Making an about me section and including plenty of information about yourself probably doesn't seem all that important to you. Let me change your mind.

Most people, when buying from an online store, are a little bit worried. They're handing over money online to a person they don't know, and they may never receive their order.

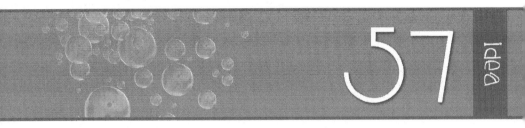

57

idea

If you put up a picture of yourself, with your name, and general information about where you live (city and state), this will ease a lot of those worries.

Also, many people enjoy shopping with a real person who has a small business, rather than a big, impersonal business. But if you're not showing them that you're a real person with a face and a name, you might as well be a big business (without the cheap prices and trust they offer).

BUY HANDMADE

Push the handmade issue. If someone is at your site and is trying to decide whether or not they'll buy your bracelet or go check out what they have to offer at Macy's, and then they see your "Buy Handmade" badge, it might spur their decision to purchase from you right then.

58

When I buy from an individual who handmade my item, it gives me warm feelings, and when I buy from a major corporation, it does not. I know many other people who feel the same way, so push that, because that's one thing you have going for your business that the big guys don't.

JEWELRY PARTIES

Remember Tupperware parties? Well, you can offer jewelry parties.

59 Idea

Ladies can book parties of 5-15 people and take catalogs and samples of your jewelry, and you can give them a commission on the amount of money they make.

JUSTIFY THEIR PURCHASE

When people buy something, they decide what they want to buy based on emotion. But they back up that decision with logic.

If they can't justify their purchase with a logical reason, they won't buy it, even if they want to. This is why sales do so well – people say, "I have to buy it now if I want to get it at this great price."

You can justify their purchase by notifying them that you only have a limited quantity, that they won't be able to find this jewelry elsewhere, that the item is very durable and will last for years, or that your special will expire soon.

TELL THEM WHERE THEY CAN WEAR IT

How many times have you nearly bought something, but then thought, "Oh, I'll probably never use it." Tell them where they can wear their new jewelry, and suddenly they'll imagine all the great times they'll be having, looking beautiful in their jewelry.

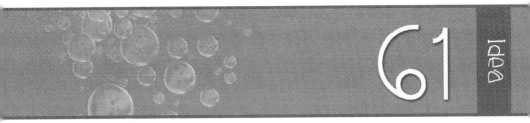

61

Idea

I have a friend who, years ago, was extremely broke. She bought a red dress that she couldn't afford because of one line in the ad. It said, "You'll look stunning on Christmas morning when you come out to unwrap presents in this elegant, red, Christmas dress."

Imagining herself on Christmas morning with family in a beautiful Christmas dress rather than the ratty pajamas she normally wore was just too much to resist. If the ad had just said, "A beautiful red a-line dress made of 90% cotton and 10% polyester," there's no way she would have bought it.

TELL THEM HOW THEY'LL FEEL

This ties into the last idea, but it's also very important in itself. I told you before that people really buy based on emotion, and then they back that up with logic. So you have to get them anticipating that emotion!

Tell them how stunning they'll feel, and how this bracelet will catch all the men's eye, or how happy and proud their daughter will be to have her first real gold necklace.

TELL THEM WHY THEY HAVE TO BUY IT NOW

Most sales don't go through because people tell themselves that they will just buy it later, or buy it for Christmas, or buy it when Annie's birthday comes around. Unfortunately, when that time rolls around, they have already forgotten about the item and your shop.

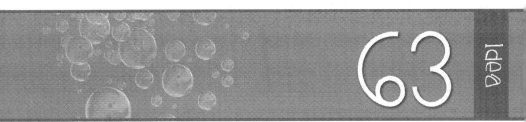

63

Idea

You have to get the sale while they're there. Run sales, tell them there is a limited quantity, or run coupons. Tell them to get it while it's there, because you won't be making more.

COLLABORATE WITH PHOTOGRAPHERS

Loan your jewelry out to photographers who can use it in their photoshoots.

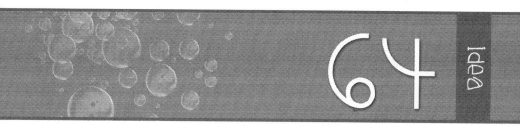

Idea 69

Now you'll have great photos of your jewelry, and the photographer has some great jewelry to use in his shoots. You can both post links to each others' sites on your sites.

JEWELRY CARDS

Design greeting cards that have a cut-out in the middle for your pendant.

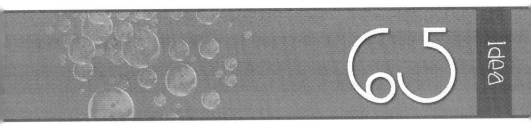

Make the design on your card match the pendant, and put the pendant on the inside of the card.

It's a gift and a card rolled into one. It's convenient, unique, and creative.

JEWELRY-WEARING MANNEQUINS

Offer to let boutiques use your jewelry on their mannequins in exchange for some free advertising.

This will work best with small, local boutiques where you can speak one-on-one with the owners.

Explain how much better the outfits on the mannequins would look with jewelry accessories.

CATALOGS

Design catalogs and give them to boutique and clothing shop owners. They would likely be willing to buy your jewelry and re-sell it in their shops.

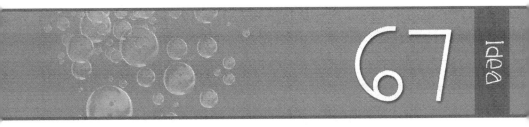

67

idea

This isn't competition for you if you only sell online, because you're targeting online shoppers around the world, while they're targeting in-store shoppers in their neighborhood.

If you mail the catalog and ship the items to the boutique, you would never even have to go in.

THE LITTLE BLACK BOXES

At thelittleblackboxes.com you can give away samples or promotions that will be sent out in little black boxes with other stores' samples to people who pay $10 for a box.

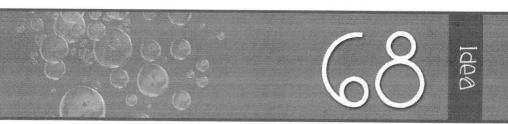

68 Idea

I've heard nothing but good things about this service, and it really does result in a big spike of traffic.

GIVE TO BARTENDERS

Where can you find massive crowds of fashion-conscious young girls with money to spend? Bars!

69

Idea

Give away or loan your jewelry to bartenders at the most popular local bars, and give them business cards to hand out to people who compliment them on their jewelry.

SCRATCH-OFFS

Here's something that's way more fun and more likely to get results than a coupon: Scratch-offs! Did you know that studies show that people who have a way to interact with your promotion are more likely to respond?

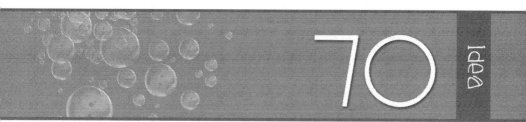

Let them scratch their ticket to get a prize or a coupon, and you're more likely to get a customer out of it.

Here's a site that offers custom scratch-off tickets: justscratchit.com

JEWELRY OF THE MONTH CLUB

Offer a gift package that sends a new piece of jewelry to the gift recipient every month.

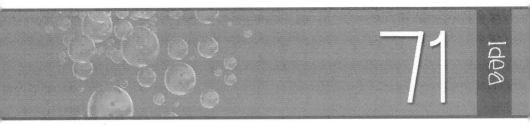

71

Idea

For the first month, you can send a package explaining their jewelry of the month gift, a message from the sender, and a calendar that tells them when they're going to get their next package.

LEARN YOUR DEMOGRAPHIC

Make polls for your website and ask questions about where your customers live, what kind of jewelry they prefer, etc. You can make free polls at misterpoll.com.

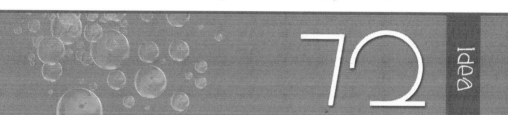

72

Idea

This will help you decide how to make your ads, coupons, and products better suit the majority of your customers.

GOOGLE IMAGE FUNCTION

Hundreds of thousands of people use the Google Image search on Google.com.

73

Idea

Make sure the title of all your jewelry images (example:emeraldbracelet.jpg) includes descriptive words about your jewelry, so people can find your jewelry by typing in "emerald bracelet" (or whatever words you're using) in Google Images. It's best to use around 4 descriptive words.

PICK YOUR BEST CUSTOMERS

Figure out which customers spend the most at your shop. Spend more on treating these customers well, because they're good customers and you don't want to lose them to a shop that will treat them better than you do.

74

Idea

Be sure and send them thank you notes, special offers, or free gifts with their orders. Make sure they know that you really appreciate their business.

ASK OPEN-ENDED QUESTIONS

Every few times you mail your newsletter, include a question asking what your customers would like to see more of.

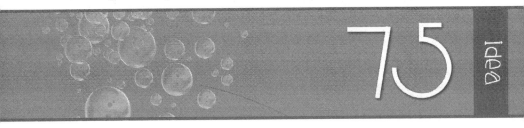

75 Idea

This is sometimes more helpful than a poll, because customers have a chance to voice their entire opinion, and give you ideas you hadn't thought of.

Ask them if there's any new style of jewelry they'd like to see, or if there's any information that would be helpful to add to the website. Most people are very willing to pipe in with their thoughts.

CREATE A YOUTUBE SLIDESHOW

Make a slideshow of your items in Windows Movie Maker or onetruemedia.com and post it on YouTube.

76 idea

Put your site address at the end of the video. This is guaranteed free traffic.

THE SOFT SELL

A lot of people aren't comfortable making promotional videos, but they are good at just being themselves. If this is the case, you can make YouTube videos, blogs, or comics that have nothing to do with your jewelry shop. They can be 100% personal and all about you.

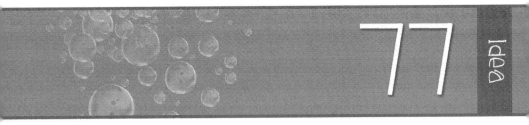

Just mention something to the side that says, "I also own a handmade jewelry shop! Check it out!" That's it!

If people like you, and they probably do if they're looking at your blog, videos, or comics, then they'll want to check out your shop, and many will want to buy from you, just because they know and like you.

STAY UP-TO-DATE

Go to Google News and type in "jewelry" every so often. Or go to the press release websites (prweb.com and prnewswire.com) and type in "jewelry."

78 Idea

This will keep you up to date on what's going on in the jewelry business world and whether or not there are any exciting fads you can implement on your own site.

It's a good idea to subscribe to celebrity and fashion magazines to stay on top of new trends.

HALF OFF FOR TESTIMONIALS

Offer a 50% off one item coupon to customers who give you a testimonial that you can use on your site. A video testimonial would be even better – you could offer 50% off two items for those.

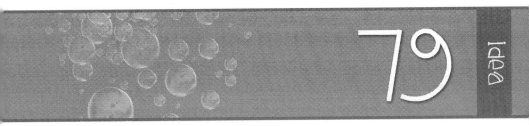

79

idea

Testimonials build trust and that's always important for an online business.

And beyond trust, they also get you exposure, if you use them to your advantage. Post video testimonials on YouTube with a link to your site.

MAKE YOUR OWN HOLIDAY

Celebrate Emerald Day or Pearl Day on your website every year and have a sale on items that have those gemstones in them. Make your front page all about Emeralds or Pearls.

Many people buy jewelry for their friends or significant others based on their birthstone, so really play it up. Put it in your newsletter and you could even add a fun horoscope to go along with the different months.

You could even have a holiday every month for each month's gemstone. January 1st would be Garnet Day, February 1st would be Amethyst Day, etc.

PROMOTIONAL MINTS

You can get your website address and your company logo custom printed on buttermints for only $30 for a case of 1,000 at 4imprint.com.

81

Idea

Bring these up in a bowl to local restaurants and tell them they can have them for free to leave out for customers.

POSTCARDS

Print postcards at vistaprint.com or overnightprints.com with pictures of your jewelry on them and your site address.

idea 82

Then leave stacks of them at libraries and bookstores and anywhere else that allows promotional materials. Hit up local boutiques and restaurants and ask if you can put your post-cards in their entry areas.

You can even leave them in the open slots at hotels that have a visitor information section that feature advertisements for

RETURN POLICY

Make sure you have an excellent return policy. I know a certain store that has a great variety of electronics, but an awful return policy, full of restrictions and re-stocking fees.

83

So I shop at a general retail store that has only a few electronics, but an excellent return policy. I have never returned an electronics item to this store, but it's very important to me know that if I'm not satisfied, I can take the item back.

That company has lost thousands of dollars off of just me alone by not offering a great return policy, and the company I shop at hasn't had to deal with one return from me, so take that into consideration when you review your return policy. The amount of customers you'll gain far outweighs the cost of returns.

TARGET SPENDERS

When deciding where to advertise, remember that unique monthly visitors is very important, but what is even more important is the quality of those visitors.

Just because a site has loads of visitors and cheap advertising doesn't mean you want to advertise there if the site attracts the wrong kind of people.

Think of who your target audience is, now think of where that target audience goes when they want to spend money. Advertise there.

GIRL SCOUT COOKIES

Offer to give a great coupon to the girl scouts to include with their cookie sales. Every time someone buys a box, they get a coupon.

85

Idea

You're targeting people who have money to spend (because they're buying cookies) and the girl scouts are getting an extra incentive to encourage people to buy from them.

The more quality, helpful information you have on your site, the higher Google ranking you'll get and the more return visitors you'll get.

86

Idea

Try to include sections like, "How to Pick the Right Gemstones for Your Skin Tone" and watch how many more of your visitors will come from Google searches instead of paid advertising.

PROJECT WONDERFUL

Project Wonderful is pay-per-impressions advertising that is really cheap. If you're just starting out in paid advertising, I highly recommend it.

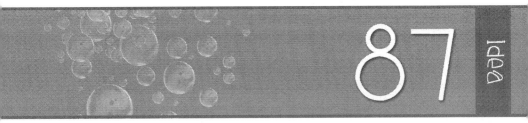

Project Wonderful has a list of sites that offer advertising spots, and you bid to get that spot. Most spots are extremely cheap (0.01-0.30), and if you're the highest bid, you appear in the spot.

There's more detailed information at their site: projectwonderful.com/advertisewithus.php

GOOGLE ADWORDS

Google Adwords is pay-per-click advertising that is extremely targeted. You choose what keywords you want to show up in when someone types them into Google.

For example, if you sell children's jewelry, you could choose the keywords, "childrens jewelry, kid jewelry, jewelry for kids." Then you choose how much you're willing to pay for each click on the ad, with a minimum of 0.05 per click.

You control how much you want to spend on each ad, how much you want to spend each day, which countries you want to see the ad, etc.

You can find more information at their site:
adwords.google.com

GOOGLE ADWORDS - PLACEMENTS

Have you ever wondered how small businesses managed to get their ad placed on huge websites like Myspace or About.com? Well this is the answer:
Google Adwords Placements.

Once you sign up for Google Adwords, go to the Placements section and choose which websites you'd like to see your text ad on. Almost every major website that offers advertising is there. It's still pay-per-click, and you can set different amounts you're willing to pay for each placement ad.

You can make video ads, audio ads, text ads, or image ads.

MAJABA

Majaba.com is a site that has a tool for Etsy sellers to see how many hearts and views their items have. It's extremely popular with Etsy sellers, and most look at it almost every day.

You can advertise on Majaba for only $15 a week, or $50 a month.

Almost all Etsy sellers are also Etsy buyers. So, if you're advertising to Etsy sellers, you're also advertising to buyers.

Many Etsians also have blogs where they feature other sellers, so if they see you on Majaba and like your things, they're likely to feature you in their blog, which is great exposure and another backlink.

HOLIDAYS

Jump on the holiday bandwagon. During Christmas, make necklaces with mistletoe on them.

91 Idea

During Halloween, make ghost earrings.

Women love to celebrate with accessories.

USP

USP means Unique Selling Position. What makes your shop unique? How are you different from all the other jewelry sellers out there?

Are your items victorian, are they ornate, are they more economical?

Figure out what your USP is and make sure you're the very best at it.

PROFESSIONAL PHOTOS

Are you about to set up shop or want to re-do all the photos
in your shop and make them look professional? If you can't
afford to go out and buy a professional camera,
you can rent one!

93 Idea

The quality of your photos makes all the difference when you
have an online shop, and especially when you're selling
jewelry, because it has so many details and it's so small.

You can rent professional digital cameras here:
dpi-digitalphoto.com/catalog.php

You could also hire a professional photographer to take your
photos for you. Try craigslist.org to find photographers, or
just do a Google search for photographers in your area.

TAKE WEIRD PHOTOS

Decorate a Christmas tree entirely with jewelry. Make a
jeweled umbrella. Make jewelry for animals.

94

Idea

People will look, people will forward it onto their friends,
people will Stumble and Digg, and you will get loads of free
traffic, just for being a bit zany.

FLOWER JEWELRY

Offer to ship jewelry stuffed into a rosebud to gift recipients with a note attached telling them they will get their surprise when the flower blooms. This would be especially popular for Valentine's Day.

95 Idea

Another option would be to make your own hollow, chocolate roses and put the jewelry inside.

SUBMIT COUPONS

There are tons of sites that list promo codes and coupons for online shops.

Submit your coupons to coupon sites like mycoupons.com and you'll see a lot more traffic for it.

The next few ideas are only applicable
to sellers who have Etsy shops.

WE LOVE ETSY

At etsylove.ning.com you can network with other Etsians and
show off your jewelry.

97 | idea

Remember that most Etsy sellers are Etsy buyers, so you're
marketing to a good audience.

IMAGE BOX PROMOS

Sometimes you can't use up all the image boxes you have available for your items.

In that case, you and other Etsians can promote each other's items in your free image boxes.

Just put some pictures of your items in the image, with the address to your etsy shop (example.etsy.com) and put them in each others' listings.

WEEKLY PRIZE DRAWING

Have a drawing every week for anyone who enters in your Etsy forum post. To enter, they just have to post a response that says, "entry."

This will keep the topic bumped up at the top for hours. Then you draw a name from the entries to determine a winner.

Will all those people looking at your posts, a lot of them are going to go look at your shop.

You can even post the prize as a listing and put the link to the listing in the forum post, so people will definitely look at your shop to see what they have a free chance to win.

THE POWER OF ONE

Every time you list a new product, it gets put on the top of the listings, making for plenty of exposure for you, but not for long. And every time someone buys something from your shop, that listing gets sent to the top of pounce, where it stays slightly longer.

100

idea

So, let's say you have 5 of the same type of bracelet. Only list that you have 1 in stock. When that one sells out, and you list another, you get exposure in the new listings *and* exposure in pounce, which sometimes results in a string of sales one right after another.

If you're wondering why you sold no items all week, and then sold 4 in a day, it was probably because of pounce.

AVATAR

If you post in the Etsy forums for marketing purposes, make
sure you have a clickable avatar.

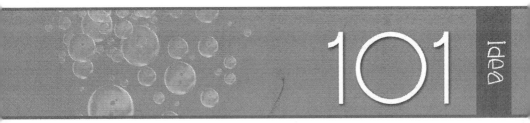

101

Idea

Your avatar should clearly show an eye-catching piece of
jewelry, of which people want to see more detail.

Don't put a picture of yourself, your shop name,
or a sale sign.

If you don't post in the forums for marketing purposes, feel
free to be creative with your avatar and include a picture of
yourself or your shop name if you like.